Niihau

Kauai

Oahu

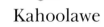
Molokai

Maui

Lanai

Kahoolawe

FROM THE SKIES OF PARADISE

MAUI

Hawaii

FROM THE SKIES OF PARADISE

MAUI

Aerial Photography by Douglas Peebles

Text by Tom Stevens

Mutual Publishing

PREVIOUS PAGE: *The dramatic Pauwalu Point headland between Keanae Peninsula and Wailua, on the Hana coast.*

4   5   6   7   8   9

Third Printing December 1996
Fourth Printing March 1999

ISBN 0-935180-74-5

Mutual Publishing
1215 Center Street, Suite 210
Honolulu, Hawaii 96816
Telephone (808) 732-1709
Fax (808) 734-4094
Email: mutual@lava.net
Url # http://www.pete.com/mutual

Printed in Taiwan by China Color

C O N T E N T S

If you could float in the air high enough, you would see that Maui takes on a human dimension.

The West Maui volcano, Puu Kukui, is the island's head. The face is turned westward toward Lanai and Molokai. The larger of the island's two volcanos, 10,000-foot Haleakala, could be termed Maui's body, with its back to the northeast trade winds and its ample Polynesian chest and stomach swelling toward Kahoolawe in the lee.

That the island is named for Polynesia's most famous demigod is widely known, but not often considered. Despite its North American institutions and Asian social influences, Maui is a Polynesian place—discovered and settled by Polynesians and named for their most appealing deity.

Maui was a restless god whose creative power and playfulness were legendary throughout the Pacific. It is said he pulled the Hawaiian Islands from the sea while fishing, that he snared the sun as it raced across the sky and ordered it to slow down. It seems fitting that the island bearing Maui's name should be associated with both creative power and playfulness.

The great natural forces that shaped the "Valley Isle"—volcanic eruptions, trade winds, ocean currents, the eternal work of water on stone—have created a place unlike any other.

The handsome Douglas Peebles photographs that follow reveal this creativity in all its wonder. Maui's playfulness is manifest as well.

The island that provided challenging surf, perilous jumping cliffs and steep ti-leaf slides for Hawaiian royalty has in recent years become a playground of another sort. The world's best windsurfers now hoist their bright sails at Kanaha, Maalaea and Hookipa. The island's golfers and tennis players enjoy facilities unmatched in the Pacific. And broad beaches with five-star resorts now cater to a new royalty—the world's wealthiest and most discriminating vacationers.

Yet Maui's Polynesian heritage remains. It is evident in its sugar, taro, and banana crops, in the relics of royal history of Hana and Lahaina, and in the unmistakable "Pacific-ness" of these high subtropical islands.

As you explore the island from aloft in these beautiful photographs, you will see places previously revealed only to the sun—now that Maui has slowed the sun's race across the sky.

Relax and enjoy. The more you look, the more you see.

CENTRAL MAUI

Central Maui used to be a desert. When Kamehameha's war canoes landed at Kahului in 1790 to battle Maui's King Kahekili, the Big Islanders had to cross "the sand hills" before driving the Maui warriors to their deaths in the steep Iao valley.

Now the former desert is a sea of sugar cane bracketed by Wailuku and Kahului on the windward (north) coast and Kihei on the south. It is the geographic, commercial and civic center of the island.

Lahaina missionary sons Samuel T. Alexander and Henry Perrine Baldwin in the 1860s bought thousands of acres in the island's central "saddle" to grow cane. They were joined in 1876 by California sugar refiner Claus Spreckels who swiftly became a confidant and poker partner of King David Kalakaua.

Spreckels lent the "Merry Monarch" and his ministers money they could not repay, then recovered it in the form of water rights in East Maui. Using a tunnel system pioneered in the Big Island's Kohala Mountains, the Maui planters used hundreds of Chinese workers from 1876 to 1878 to build the 30-mile Hamakua Ditch system. Damming a score of streams on the windward slopes of Haleakala, they diverted 50 million gallons a day to Central Maui, where it continues to irrigate thousands of acres of sugar cane as part of a 74-mile system that today can deliver 450 million gallons a day.

Spreckels fell from royal favor and his name today figures only in the Central Maui settlement of Spreckelsville, a one-time plantation camp that fronts what must be the world's best windsurfing coast. But Alexander & Baldwin (A&B) became synonymous with Maui. The firm and its

PREVIOUS PAGES: *Sugar remains king in Central Maui a century after planters tapped East Maui streams to water the arid "saddle." Alexander & Baldwin's HC&S plantation, pictured here, stretches 36,000 acres from the flanks of Haleakala to distant West Maui.*

LEFT: *Wailuku town fans from the mouth of Iao Valley along the West Maui Mountains. Flanking the town are Wailuku Agribusiness sugar fields (left) and macadamia nut orchards (right). The Maui County building is in the center.*

subsidiaries ran sugar mills at Paia and Puunene, the harbor at Kahului, and plantation camps stretching along a railroad from Haiku to what is now Kahului town.

Henry Baldwin also bought Haleakala Ranch on the western slopes of the big volcano. His descendents today control more than 30,000 acres stretching up from Wailea, a resort developed from 10,000 acres owned by an A&B subsidiary, Matson Navigation Co.

While A&B was converting Central Maui into prosperous sugar plantations, another set of missionary descendants built dams, tunnels and ditches to collect streamwater from the verdant but sparsely populated valleys of the West Maui mountains. These were once tiered and planted in taro, bananas and sweet potato by Hawaiian farmers before diseases introduced by European explorers, American whalers and Chinese laborers had felled two of every three Hawaiians.

Under C. Brewer & Co. management, Wailuku Sugar planted cane; now the northern acreage is in macadamia nuts, the southern in pineapple, and the firm is known as Wailuku Agribusiness. Golf courses and luxury homes with panoramic views of Haleakala command the slopes above those fields.

Once a small harbor community and cattle-drive terminus nicknamed "Port Town," Kahului came into its own in the 1950s, when A&B started putting its old campsites back into sugar production. As each rickety wooden camp fell before the bulldozers, its residents got an unprecedented offer: they could buy new homes off of the plantation. Thus was born "Dream City," one of America's first fully planned residential communities.

Haleakala's smaller and older brother, Puu Kukui (candlenut hill), once soared nearly 7,000 feet. Now eroded, the sheer, mile-deep valleys have the nickname, "Yosemite of the Pacific." Running laterally are Iao stream and Iao road.

The sister cities of Wailuku (left) and Kahului form Central Maui's residential and commercial hub. Flanking the older city of Wailuku are the pineapple fields (lower left) and macadamia nut orchards (upper left) of Wailuku Agribusiness, formerly Wailuku Sugar Co. Kahului extends in concentric loops inland from the Kahului breakwater and harbor (center right), hence the town's nickname "Port Town."

15

OPPOSITE: *Hugging the wooded slopes above the Wailuku Agribusiness pineapple and sugar fields are the handsome view homes of Wailuku Heights, offering cool air and spectacular views of Haleakala.*

ABOVE: *Waikapu is considered to be Maui's most beautiful valley. Pineapple fields flank the valley and curve down toward the Maui Tropical Plantation in center foreground. Wailuku Heights is at upper right; peaceful Waikapu at lower right.*

ABOVE: *Scenic but treacherous Kahakuloa Road snakes through emerald pastures and across crumbling cliff faces north of the verdant seaside town of Waihee. Ranchlands here are among Hawaii's most scenic; the coastline among its least accessible. Small islands offshore shelter raucous seabird populations.*

OPPOSITE: *Maui's dramatic northeast coast includes deep ravines, emerald pastures, waterfalls hundreds of feet high and a memorable view of Haleakala. This region, reminiscent of California's Big Sur coastline, is dotted with family ranches atop high bluffs.*

PREVIOUS PAGES: *Once the island's major plantation town, then the home of Maui's elite, Spreckelsville is now favored by windsurfers, who sail off into the world's best wind and waves.*

ABOVE: *Rustic Paia town has become a magnet for windsurfers. Once home to 15,000 workers, Upper Paia (distance) and Lower Paia (foreground) have shrunk as HC&S plowed old camp sites back into sugar production. Baldwin Avenue (left center) leads to Haleakala.*

OPPOSITE: *The world's top windsurfers prefer the booming surf and tricky currents of Hookipa Beach Park. Major international windsurfing contests are held at Hookipa in October and April. A line of trees (at top) marks Holomua Road and the former planta-tion town of Hamakuapoko.*

OPPOSITE: *Smoke from a cane fire rises from sugar plantation fields near Puunene. These flash fires, usually lasting about 10 minutes, quickly burn off the leaves helping to make processing easier by reducing foliage.*

LEFT: *Before tourism, real estate development and windsurfing, Hawaii had "King Sugar." The industry really came into its own in the 1860s, when America's Civil War blockades cut off Southern sugar from world markets. HC&S plantation today has 36,000 acres in production and employs 1,200 workers.*

OPPOSITE: *A low isthmus of sand and pickleweed separates shallow Kealia Pond (right) from the broad expanse of Maalaea Bay. A natural basin for floodwater runoffs from Haleakala, 500-acre Kealia Pond is a federal bird sanctuary and an important wetland ecosystem. Berm-en-closed ponds (at center right) mark experimental shrimp and baitfish projects authorized by the state and county governments.*

ABOVE: *At the leeward, southern end of Central Maui is old Maalaea fishing village, today a retirement community with a string of condominiums. Skirting the base of the West Maui Mountains, Honoa-piilani Highway runs from Wailuku to Kapalua.*

WEST MAUI

West Maui is where mountains, sugar and shoreline are close together. Here Olowalu Stream (darker foliage) bisects the Puu Kukui volcano. Olowalu Valley has ancient Hawaiian petroglyphs. Sugar fields are part of the Pioneer Mill plantation.

PREVIOUS PAGES: *West Maui is where mountains, sugar and shoreline are close together. Here Olowalu Stream (darker foliage) bisects the Puu Kukui volcano. Olowalu Valley has ancient Hawaiian petroglyphs. Sugar fields are part of the Pioneer Mill plantation.*

OPPOSITE: *Sunny Lahaina has figured in island history for more than 300 years. Favored first by royalty, then by whalers and missionaries, Lahaina today is one of the world's playgrounds. Lahaina's center is its small boat harbor, with the red-roofed Pioneer Inn (at left).*

West Maui, the island's undisputed historical, tourist and recreation center, includes Olowalu, Lahaina, the Kaanapali resort area, the towns of Honokowai, Kahana and Napili, and the Kapalua resort. Lahaina is the civic and commercial hub.

So popular with Hawaiian royalty were Lahaina's calm waters, surfing beaches and smoldering evening skies that they made the town a regular vacation spot as early as the seventeenth century. King Kamehameha the Great in 1802 built a "brick palace" in Lahaina, the first western-style building in Hawaii.

Between 1810 and 1840 Lahaina was the unofficial capital of Hawaii, a distinction it lost in 1840 when Kamehameha III moved to Honolulu.

What did royalty see in Lahaina? In the lee of both Haleakala and Puu Kukui, Lahaina enjoys Hawaii's sunniest and calmest climate. While it rarely rains in the town, the lofty West Maui Mountains ensure a steady supply of fresh water.

Later, Lahaina became a favorite port for the whalers, hosting as many as 400 ships a year during the 1840-1860 peak North Pacific whaling period. The crews came ashore for grog, clean laundry, hot food, music, dancing and sport. In 1825 alone, Lahaina had 23 grog shops.Lahaina Prison did a brisk business whenever the whalers were in town.

Arriving in Lahaina in 1823, New England missionaries embarked on a 50-year tug-of-war with the whalers for the town's soul, finally

prevailing only after the discovery of petroleum had knocked the bottom out of the sperm oil trade.

In the interim, missionaries like the Rev. William Richards and the Rev. Dwight Baldwin sought to prevail upon Maui's rulers to outlaw liquor sales and rowdyism, and to keep island women off the whaling ships. These measures prompted occasional riots. The whalers at one point bombarded a missionary home with cannonballs.

As whaling died out, sugar, pineapple and cattle ranching became significant in West Maui's economy. Pioneer Inn, Maui's first hotel, went up in Lahaina in 1902, but the visitor-industry boom was still generations away.

Tourism was accepted by West Maui shortly before Statehood in 1959. Gambling that cheap trans-Pacific jet fares to the new 50th State would attract visitors who eventually could be lured away from Waikiki, Pioneer Mill's parent firm, American Factors (Amfac), created along three miles of previously little used coast Hawaii's first master-planned destination resort—Kaanapali.

With exemplary foresight, Amfac's design team and Lahaina residents decided to put Lahaina's new resort industry outside the town itself which was to remain a low-rise historic district of restored landmark structures, small shops and restaurants. The Lahaina Restoration Foundation was formed in 1963 to carry out this vision.

As a result, Lahaina today boasts of many handsomely restored treasures, among them the old prison (1852), the seamen's hospital (1830), the Hale Pai printing museum (1834), the Wo Hing Temple (1912), the Baldwin House Museum (1838), Lahainaluna High School dating from 1831 (the first school west of the Rockies), and the town's two-story court house (1859).

West Maui's most striking landmark is the rugged Kahakuloa monolith, (left), Maui's Gibraltar. The old Hawaiian village of Kahakuloa, once a self-sufficient community of taro farmers and fishermen, is gradually losing people to the easier life of Wailuku and Lahaina. Kahakuloa Stream is one of the few on Maui not dammed for sugar cultivation.

OPPOSITE: *Lahaina's westward exposure provides residents and visitors with splendid views of the sun sinking behind Lanai Island. Lahaina justly earns its nickname "The Sunset Side of Maui."*

ABOVE: *Among West Maui's assets are its vast, "calm lee" and clear views of other nearby islands. Here cloud-capped Lanai lies on a flat blue sea nine miles from Lahaina. In the foreground is Lahainaluna High School, built in 1831.*

FOLLOWING PAGES: *The warm, cobalt-blue water of the Ka'anapali coast turns to turquoise-green as it slides over the soft, white sands fronting the Sheraton Maui Ka'anapali Beach Resort. Poised on the legendary lava formation called Black Rock or Pu'u Keka'a, this newly renovated, luxury hotel boasts 510 guest rooms and suites spread out among six low-rise buildings. An immense ocean front swimming lagoon with lava-rock waterways meanders 142 yards through lush tropical landscaping, enchanting bridges, and a soothing open-air spa.*

ABOVE: *Framed by the resort coast on the left and Pioneer Mill sugar fields on the right, Kaanapali's championship golf courses host major national and international tournaments each winter. Hotels in the left foreground include the Hyatt and Marriott resorts. Visible across the channel (at the right) is Molokai, Hawaii's fifth largest island.*

OPPOSITE: *West Maui's resort coast continues north of Kaanapali past the former village of Kahana (right) toward Napili (far left). Condominiums and apartment blocks along Maui's northwest coast house Kaanapali hotel workers and vacationing "second home" owners from all over the world.*

PREVIOUS PAGES: *Developed in the late 1970s and throughout the 1980s from former pineapple and ranch lands, the 750-acre Kapalua Resort enjoys one of Hawaii's most scenic settings. The 194-room Kapalua Bay Hotel is* the flagship of a residential and recreation complex marketed to an elite clientele. Offerings include annual wine and gourmet food symposia, classical music recitals and celebrity golf and tennis tournaments.

ABOVE: *Some of Hawaii's most scenic and challenging holes of golf are to be found amid Kapalua's championship layouts, including these formidably guarded "mauka" (mountain) fairways carved from former pineapple fields. A one-time Honolua Plantation "punawai" (irrigation pond) has been incorporated here as a water hazard. Dark evergreens (at right) are Norfolk Island pines.*

A sightseeing helicopter hovers before spectacular Honokohau Falls, one of many West Maui cataracts that continue to erode the ancient Puu Kukui volcano. The mountain's deep, jungled ravines gave Maui its nickname "The Valley Isle." Helicopter tours are popular with visitors but not with isle residents.

PREVIOUS PAGES: *"Maui's Gibraltar,"* lofty monolithic *Kahakuloa Head, divides West Maui from Central Maui and guards the Hawaiian village at its base. The refurbished Protestant Church stands at right. Kahakuloa is the home of Maui's most famous falsetto singers, Sol and Richard Hoopii. Becalmed in this photo, the bay (at left) thunders with 20-foot surf in winter.*

LEFT: *A rare cloudless day atop Puu Kukui (West Maui) volcano reveals the extraordinary Eke Crater, a mile-high plateau whose marshy center is a botanical wonderland of miniature Hawaiian plants.*

UPCOUNTRY

Upcountry Maui, or "Cloud Country" to its residents, is the windward flank of Haleakala volcano from the coastal foothills to the 10,023-foot-high crater rim.

In this region of vast ranches, small farms and storybook villages, the land is green or gold by turns, its rolling pastures striped with darker rows of windbreak trees. Clouds run before the trade winds like galleons under sail, setting off the deep, sharp blue of the Upcountry sky.

The crisp and clear air affords peerless views of West Maui, Kahoolawe, Lanai, Molokai and, on extraordinary days, Oahu. Few other places in the world command such a panorama.

At night, the heavens over Upcountry Maui shimmer. Far from city lights, telescopes on Haleakala crater's rim explore our own and other galaxies, and Air Force laser weapons scan the skies .

In the rich volcanic Upcountry soil, particularly in the Kula farming belt, vegetables and flowers flourish in a unique range of altitude, weather and temperature conditions. Kula onions are so sweet they can be eaten like apples.

Farther east, at the windward edge of the mountain, lie dairy farms, deep ravines, thickets of wild guava, and fragrant eucalyptus forests. Pineapples march in orderly ranks from Olinda to Omaopio, sugar fields stretch from Haiku past Pulehu.

Cattle graze in the thick grass of scenic Haleakala Ranch, Kaanaolu Ranch, Erehwon ("nowhere" spelled backward), and breathtaking Ulupalakua Ranch, site of Maui's award-winning Erdman-Tedeschi winery.

PREVIOUS PAGES: *Upcountry sunrises and sunsets are the most spectacular in Hawaii. For sunrise, that means the summit of Haleakala well before dawn. Here the Big Island's Mauna Kea and Mauna Loa are visible above the clouds.*

Once part of the Baldwin family's vast Haleakala Ranch, the mountain's spectacular "crater" was traded to the federal government for park use in the 1920s. A line of cinder cones pocks the arid top half of the crater, which has well maintained hiking trails and cabins for overnight camping.

Further downslope, the fast-growing communities of Haiku, Makawao, Pukalani and Kula attract new residents willing to trade commuting for open space and country life.

Sparsely populated previously (the Hawaiians preferred warmer, wetter coastal valleys), Upcountry Maui in the nineteenth century was settled by Chinese and Japanese farmers. Later, Portuguese came from the Madeira and Azores Islands.

During California goldrush days, the Chinese at Keokea raised potatoes and did laundry for the forty-niners! Later they participated in Asian history by sheltering the family of Chinese revolutionary Sun Yat Sen.

The Portuguese who reached Maui found the bracing Upcountry climate and rolling rangelands eerily familiar; they duplicated in almost every respect their volcanic Atlantic-island home. Skilled in animal husbandry, masonry, construction and agriculture, the Portuguese have shaped every aspect of Upcountry life.

As elsewhere in the islands, missionary descendants—Baldwins, Rices, Castles, Cookes, Campbells, Damons, Athertons, Alexanders, Doles, Judds, Binghams and their "calabash cousins"—left their mark Upcountry as ranchers and landowners.

While Upcountry is viewed from the air less often than Maui's sea level regions, one band of adventurers has seen it more clearly than most. Pushing off from the crater rim itself on still days, hang-gliders are often seen in the soft morning air over Kula. In the rural quiet, farm workers can hear the hang glider pilots talking high overhead.

"O Linda Vista" (oh, beautiful view) was the first Spanish-speaking visitor's summation of this region, or so an old story goes. Blessed with ample rainfall and scudding trade winds, Olinda remains a storybook quilt of pastures, windbreak rows and farm lots. This southerly view includes the lush pastures of Haleakala Dairy (center), the scenic gemstone of 30,000-acre Haleakala Ranch.

RIGHT: *Flanked by HC&S sugar fields (left) and Maui Land and Pineapple Co. fields (foreground), the Pukalani Golf Course surrounds some of Maui's most sought-after real estate.*

OPPOSITE: *Crater Road zig-zags toward Haleakala's 10,023-foot summit through the high pastures and windbreak tree lines of Haleakala Ranch. Owned by descendants of Protestant missionary Dwight Baldwin, the 30,000-acre spread is Maui's largest ranch. More than a million travelers a year drive to Haleakala National Park, once part of the ranch.*

PREVIOUS PAGES: *Enjoying some of the best viewing conditions this side of deep space, Haleakala's 18-acre "Science City" harbors University of Hawaii and U.S. Air Force installations off-limits to the public. At night a green laser ranging beam is fired from Science City to a mirror dish left on the moon by Apollo astronauts.*

ABOVE: *As it nears the volcano's rim, Crater Road forks to offer a breathtaking vista at Kalahaku Overlook (left) or an equally astonishing view from the park visitor center (to the right). Faintly visible just below the crater's far rim is the Sliding Sands foot trail, which leads to three cabins built in the 1930s along the park's 21-mile circumference.*

OPPOSITE: *A dozen waterfalls thread the sheer windward face of a Haleakala cliff. These falls at Manawainui helped carve one of the high, "hanging valleys" that characterize the volcano's "weather" side. Some falls are broken into steps, with a pool at each level.*

OPPOSITE: *Haleakala's windward rim falls off in precipitous, cloud-hung valleys laced with waterfalls. Jungled valleys like Kipahulu harbor some of Hawaii's rare native birds and plants.*

LEFT: *A rare cloudless day permitted this remarkable view into the crater. Rain forests mantle the sharp ridges and gorges that once funneled lava flows to the sea.*

ABOVE: *Kaupo Ranch at the base of one of Haleakala's two great "gaps" can also qualify as "Upcountry" Maui. Lava pulsing down Kaupo Gap created verdant pastures. Hikers can descend 10 miles from the crater floor to the ocean via a trail crossing Kaupo Ranch.*

OPPOSITE: *Founded as a sugar plantation in the 1840s, Ulupalakua became a cattle ranch in 1856. In 1974, the scenic ranch diversified into wine production and sheep raising.*

Velvety meadows of Ulupalakua (literally, "bread-fruit ripening place") roll off toward the distant Pacific with fairy-tale beauty. The area may have got its name because breadfruit unloaded at Makena ripened by the time they were carried miles upslope to Ulupalakua.

HANA COAST

East Maui often is simply called the Hana Coast after its most famous town.

While the "birthplace of royalty" has seen as much history as any part of Hawaii, its extraordinary beauty is what sets the Hana Coast apart. This is what visitors think of as "Hawaii." Majestic cliffs dive hundreds of feet into a cobalt-blue sea. There are few reefs and shallows. This is open ocean, dark and deep.

The land, green in all shades, rises steeply into cool gray clouds. Pierced by sharp ridges, the clouds rain down into forests of ohia, bamboo, monkeypod and hala and pelt the wide leaves of taro, banana and tree-climbing monstera.

Streams fill and race toward the sea, thundering through the jungle from cataract to pool. Even after 450 million gallons of rain a day pours into the ditches and tunnels of the East Maui Irrigation Co., hundreds of millions of gallons still tumble into the ocean.

Facing northeast, directly into Hawaii's trade winds, the Hana Coast vies with north Kauai and the Big Island's Hamakua Coast as the rainiest spot in the Pacific.

To the east of Kailua lie the picturesque Hawaiian towns of Keanae and Wailua, the former on a peninsula formed when lava flowed down Haleakala's Koolau Gap. Taro farming is still practiced in Keanae, which also boasts a 135-year-old Congregational church and a YMCA camp that can be rented for three-night stays. Near the camp is the Keanae Arboretum, a showcase of taro and other native plants.

PREVIOUS PAGES: *The 80-year-old Hana "Highway," here snakes along the cliffs above Honomanu Bay (right). Skirting steep gorges and clinging to cliff faces, the road twists more than 50 miles and has 56 bridges, 600 curves, and numerous roadside swimming holes and waterfalls.*

OPPOSITE: *Residual mists from a passing cloud trace a faint rainbow across remote Waihoi Valley, an ancient lava flow purling from Haleakala crater (upper right) toward Seven Pools east of Hana. Guarded by vast escarpments and generally inhospitable weather, Waihoi Valley remains one of the last unspoiled habitats for rare Hawaiian bird and plant species.*

Wailua also has taro farms, some of the most beautiful lawns in the Pacific, and a Catholic shrine (Our Lady of Fatima) built in 1860 with coral blocks pitched up out of the ocean by a freak storm. When Protestants went to gather some of the coral for their church, the story goes, the ocean took it back again with a huge wave.

Other dramatic features of the Keanae-Wailua area are Honomanu Bay and valley, the latter leading to 3,000-foot cliffs and a 1,000-foot waterfall. The sheltered bay, with its dark sand and flowering jungle trees, is a favorite winter surf spot when other breaks are "blown out" (too windy). It reminds many travelers of Polynesia.

Past wayside parks, waterfalls and icy swimming holes lie Hana and its outlying villages. The enormous Piilanihale Heiau near Nahiku bespeaks this area's importance to the Hawaiians, who built this terraced stone temple complex in the 1500s. Blessed with abundant rainfall, excellent fishing and rich soil, the Hana Coast once had a population numbering in the thousands.

Further east lie white sand swimming beaches at Koki and Hamoa, the splendid cliffs and freshwater pools of Kipahulu, and the rugged ranchlands of Kaupo. As the island "turns the corner" from windward to leeward in this stretch, you pass from dense rain forests to cactus-studded badlands in less than 10 miles.

A steep waterfall high above Hana attests to the erosive grandeur of Hawaii's prevailing trade winds, which annually release hundreds of millions of gallons onto Haleakala's jungly northeast slopes. Treacherous topography and dense foliage make dozens of waterfalls and hundreds of freshwater pools inaccessible to all but the hardiest mountaineers.

OPPOSITE: *Hana Coast waters are deep cobalt blue, since the land plunges steeply to great depths. Fishing and diving are excellent, but access is hazardous, and sudden high surf has taken lives.*

ABOVE: *A "twin falls" tumbles into the ocean, forming a shallow pool where salt and fresh water meet. This remote East Maui region has long valued fishing, hunting and farming skills more than money. Unlike in this photo, rainy days far outnumber clear ones along this coast.*

OPPOSITE: *The only peninsula along Maui's east coast, Kaenae was formed by an eruption that sent lava from Haleakala Crater down the steep Koolau Gap (in the distance). Family homes, taro farms and the 1856 Congregational Church (left foreground) dot the leaf-shaped peninsula.*

ABOVE: *On this outcrop between Nahiku and Hana, the great Piilanihale Heiau (temple) was built 500 years ago by the descendents of Piilani, a king who unified Maui's warring districts. The main temple complex is the bare rock structure edging into the jungle at right.*

LEFT: *One of Hana's most popular features is Waianapanapa State Park, which fronts a bay of scalloped coves and black sand beaches. Fishermen have long netted schools of akule (mackerel) in this bay, which "booms" as breaking waves trap air in shoreline caves.*

FOLLOWING PAGES: *Kauiki Head, birthplace of the power-ful Queen Kaahumanu and the site of ancient battles between Maui and Hawaii kings, overlooks Hana town (right) and the verdant pas-tures of 4,500-acre Hana Ranch. Just visible emerging from the shadow (at center) is the Hana wharf.*

77

OPPOSITE: *Craggy, surf-battered Alau Island guards the Koki white sand beach (surfline at right center) and the mirror-calm Hamoa fishing shallows at left. The island "corners" here, as shown by a confluence of ocean swells from different directions.*

ABOVE: *Tucked into the Hana Coast like a pearl is Hamoa Beach (right foreground), once the sole preserve of wealthy Hotel Hana Maui guests but now open to the general public as well. Scenic coastal ranch estates march southeast from here to Kipahulu.*

OPPOSITE: *The seven pools of Oheo Gulch and the waterfalls that feed them are among Maui's best-loved scenic features. Once poised to build a lavish resort hotel here, New York's Rockerfeller family was prevailed upon to leave the land in conservation use.*

ABOVE: *The forested upper slopes of Kaupo yield superb views of the "Big Island" of Hawaii, whose 13,000-foot volcanic summits Mauna Kea (left) and Mauna Loa (right), are visible in the middle distance. The Alenuihaha Channel separating Maui from Hawaii is regarded by mariners as the archipelago's most* punishing. *Visible above the cloud line at the channel's edge are the smaller Big Island peaks of Kohala Mountain (left) and Hualalai (right).*

ABOVE: *As Maui curves away from the trade winds, the green slopes of distant Kipahulu and Kaupo give way to the arid badlands of Kahikinui ("Great Tahiti"), once a major Hawaiian settlement. This road goes from rain forest to cactus desert in minutes.*

OPPOSITE: *Kaupo Church (center) and the Kaupo Ranch beyond mark the end of East Maui's "green" side. Hikers reach this point after a 20-mile, 10,000-foot descent from the summit of Haleakala. The Kaupo peninsula formed when lava poured out Haleakala's Kaupo Gap.*

SOUTH MAUI

South Maui waited centuries for fresh water. When the water arrived, this "15-mile town without a center" became the fastest-growing region in the state. It includes two wealthy resort communities, Wailea and Makena, plus Maalaea and Kihei inhabited by a mix of retirees, tourists and working people. Cactus, beaches, hotels and golf courses line the streets.

Until 30 years ago this hot, dry, remote, dusty, mesquite-lined stretch of coast was, like Kaanapali, considered to be suitable mainly for fishing and camping. It had a single dirt road, a few fishing people, some Haleakala Ranch cowboys, two small stores, and a gas pump.

When 1959 brought statehood, Maui landowners started sketching resort plans for the island's sun-baked leeward coasts. But while Kaanapali's growth was planned carefully on a 25-year timetable, South Maui grew explosively. In a single decade, a hundred condominiums, hotels, mini-malls, car lots, burger stands and curio shops rose along its shoreline.

The South Maui boom continues today as the community grows away from the beaches up the gentle leeward flank of Haleakala. With zoning already in place for 250,000 residents, South Maui may one day rival Honolulu as Hawaii's largest urban area.

Among Kihei's few historic structures are the ruins of the 1853 Kalepolepo Congregational Church, last pastored by the noted Hawaiian scholar David Malo, and remains of the 200-foot-long Kihei Wharf, once used to offload Maui cargo when high seas closed the island's north shore. The wharf served interisland packets until 1915.

PREVIOUS PAGES: *Maui's youngest and fastest-growing community is the South Maui "gold coast" sun belt, here shown from the Wailea end of Maalaea Bay. Distant West Maui looks like a separate island from this angle.*

OPPOSITE: *While Maui's Kanaha-to-Hookipa coast is more famous for its wave sailing and slalom conditions, Maui windsurfers also enjoy the flatwater speed runs offered by Maalaea Bay. Some of the world's fastest open-ocean speedsailing records have been set in this howling corridor of offshore winds between Maalaea Harbor (top right) and Kihei.*

Further south, the small shoreline community of Makena boasts the 130-year-old Keawalai Congregational Church. One of the state's best-preserved Hawaiian fishing villages, Moanakala, is a few miles down the road at Cape Kinau.

Much of South Maui's history is still ahead of it, as evidenced by the growth of the 1,500-acre Wailea destination resort and luxury residential projects. With four major hotels, three championship golf courses, restaurants, a shopping center and several top-drawer condominium projects, Wailea has joined Kaanapali and Kapalua in the rarified company of world-class resorts.

The next entry may be the Seibu Corporation's Makena Resort, whose first hotel, the Maui Prince, rose in the mid-1980s south of the historic village of Makena Landing.

Beyond the Maui Prince lies Maui's most illustrious and arguably its most popular beach, Oneloa or Big Beach. Its isolation, deep yellow sand and tourquoise water drew hippies to Makena (misspelled "McKenna" in countless postcards home) during the late 1960s and 1970s, an invasion accommodated but not always appreciated by long-time Maui residents.

Adjoining Big Beach at the base of the distinctive Puu Olai (Red Hill) cinder cone is sheltered "Little Beach," whose fame as an unauthorized nude bathing area has provided Mauians with more than 20 years of spirited debate. Both beaches are scheduled for inclusion in a future state park.

While not physically a part of South Maui, half-submerged Molokini Island is a major feature. Snorkel and dive cruises from Maalaea and Kihei small-boat harbors transport thousands of visitors to the clear waters of Molokini's lagoon for undersea viewing.

PREVIOUS PAGES: *Anchored sailboats dot the flat morning water off Kamaole I Beach Park, one of three Kihei beaches the Maui county government wisely preserved for public use in the 1970s. Makena's Puu Olai cinder cone is visible at top right, and Ulupalakua Ranch at upper left.*

RIGHT: *A series of scalloped white sand beaches along Haleakala's southwestern shore marks the Wailea Resort, developed in the 1970s and 1980s from 10,000 acres of former Matson Navigation Co. ranch land. The sunny resort complex today boasts four world-class hotels, three championship golf courses and thousands of luxury con-dominium units. Wailea is Alexander & Baldwin's legacy in the Hawaii destination resort sweepstakes. In the distance at left is the town of Kihei.*

ABOVE: *The Grand Wailea Resort, Hotel & Spa nestles between the slopes of majestic Mount Haleakala and the white sandy beaches of Maui's Southern shore. The resort features a wedding chapel, waterways and gardens, a children's facility, a grand spa, and a museum-quality art collection.*

OPPOSITE: *The Puu Olai (Red Hill) cinder cone cradles "Little Beach," with Makena's Big Beach (Oneloa) sweeping toward the distant black lava peninsula of Cape Kinau and La Perouse Bay. South Maui's developed shoreline ended at Puu Olai in 1990. Kaanapali Beach once looked like this.*

OPPOSITE: *Once zoned for resorts, Makena Beach, Maui's last undeveloped beach was acquired for a state park in the late 1980s after a 15-year fight. The base of Puu Olai cinder cone is at top left, flanked by scrubland.*

ABOVE: *Maui's most recent (1790) lava flows surround La Perouse Bay, named for the French explorer who landed here in 1786, is situated on the barren "back" side of Haleakala.*

MOLOKAI
LANAI
KAHOOLAWE

PREVIOUS PAGES: *Rising as high as 2,000 feet, the shear ocean cliffs of Molokai's north shore are among the world's most spectacular. The deep valleys guarded by these cliffs are accessible to boaters during the calm summer months, but huge surf and ferocious currents close the coast in winter. Overland access is by slippery, treacherous ridge crest foot trails.*

OPPOSITE: *One of Molokai's ancient fish ponds, now choked with silt and mangroves, is visible along the Friendly Isle's leeward coast. Ocean fish were lured in through one-way gates, then fattened in shallow ponds like this one. Kaunakakai town, Molokai's largest, can be seen in the middle distance.*

W hile politics and proximity today link Maui with her sister islands Kahoolawe, Lanai and Molokai, Maui County's four islands can claim a geological connection as well. When they emerged from the ocean nearly a million years ago, one theory holds, the four islands formed a single land mass.

Like today's Big Island, that ancient "super-Maui" was built upon five major volcanoes: Haleakala and Puu Kukui of present-day Maui, Puu o Hoku and Maunaloa of what is now Molokai, and Lanaihale of what is today Lanai. As that vast island was carried northward away from its formative "hot spot" in the earth's crust, the seamount beneath it gradually subsided, and the ocean flooded the various low-lying "saddles" between the peaks.

Thus today we see four islands where once there was one (Kahoolawe is thought to be a distant outcrop of Haleakala, rather than a separate volcanic entity). This configuration is unique in the mid-Pacific, giving Maui and her sister isles a kinship that is more than visual.

Two of the islands—Kahoolawe and Lanai—even share similar weather patterns. Lying in the vast "wind shadow" of Haleakala, these relatively low neighbors catch very little rain as Hawaii's northeasterly trades expend most of their moisture on Maui. Kahoolawe and Lanai are thus "dry" islands whose usefulness was limited in Hawaiian times to fishing, temporary shelter and navigational roles. But both were important spiritually: Kahoolawe as a link to ancestral Tahiti; Lanai as a dwelling

MOLOKAI

LANAI

KAHOOLAWE

place of dangerous spirits and evil beings (akua) banished only when the Maui prince Kaululaau applied sticky gum to their eyelids as they slept.

While Kahoolawe still lacks a fresh water source and remains uninhabited today, a vigorous forestation project begun on Lanai a century ago enables that once-arid island to "wick" its water supply from the clouds that crown 3,000-foot Lanaihale. Purchased from the Territorial Government in 1920 by former Kansas farmer James Dole, Lanai subsequently became one of the world's most efficient pineapple plantations and home to 2,500 residents. As pine production increases overseas, the privately owned island is retooling as an upscale tourist resort.

Pineapple cultivation ceased altogether on Molokai in the late 1970s, but that loftier island's plentiful water supply makes diversified agriculture a possible alternative to resort development in the future. Prominent historically for its fierce warriors and powerful priests, Molokai has more recently supported cattle ranching, fishing, a large Hawaiian homestead presence, and the famed Hansen's Disease colony and hospital at Kalaupapa. The island has about 5,000 residents.

While Maui's three sister islands are nominally a part of the Maui County political structure, outside entities have an equal or greater say in each sibling's future. Kahoolawe's fate is controlled by the federal government, which has used the island as a bombing and shelling target since 1940. Dole successor Castle & Cooke owns 98 percent of Lanai and thus determines what happens there. And Molokai's large contingent of native Hawaiians gives the state and federal governments a vital stake in that island's economic and social welfare.

One of Molokai's principal exports during the great post-statehood building boom was sand, and much of it came from the three-mile-long Papohaku, beach pictured here, on the Friendly Isle's west end. Closed to the public for generations by Molokai Ranch, Papohaku is today zoned for resort and residential development. A sand mining pit is visible at the center of this photo.

ABOVE: *Isolated from "topside"
Molokai by 1,200-foot cliffs
and formidable surf much of
the year, low-lying Kalaupapa
Peninsula houses the Hansen's
Disease (leprosy) settlement
made famous by the Belgian
priest Father Damien de
Veuster a century ago. Fewer*
*than 100 patients remain at
the settlement, which has its
own landing strip, barge
harbor and water system.*

OPPOSITE: *Hawaii's last fully
functioning plantation town
is Lanai City, which houses
all of the island's 2,500 residents. Surrounded by pineapple fields, pastures and lofty
Cook Island pines, the quaint,
geometric town is a neighborly
place with as many dogs and*
*roosters as automobiles.
Lanai's 3,000-foot volcano,
Lanaihale, rises behind
the town.*

RIGHT: *At the vanguard of Lanai's move from an agricultural economy to a tourist-based economy is the Lodge at Koele, the first of several world-class resorts to be developed on the former "Pineapple Isle." The hotel features gourmet cookery and butler service for each suite.*

OPPOSITE: *There is no shortage of white sand beaches on Lanai. Here on the island's arid west end, access to the beach is by sea or by jeep road only. Lanai's shallow reefs and extraordinary "pinnacle" coral formations are popular destinations for scuba and snorkel charters from Lahaina, a mere nine miles distant.*

The reddish clay "hardpan" characteristic of Kahoolawe's summit is clearly evident in this photo, which also shows the Target Island's formidable cliffs and numerous gullies. While the island remains under U.S. Navy control, successful court actions during the 1980s won Hawaiian advocacy groups an important role in future planning for the island. On a clear day, you can see five other islands from Kahoolawe—Hawaii, Maui, Lanai, Molokai and Oahu. Here West Maui (left side) and Haleakala (right) overlook the Target Island's sheer ocean cliffs.

Maui's most recent (1790) lava flows surround La Perouse Bay, named for the French explorer who landed here in 1786. Situated on the barren "back" side of Haleakala, Cape Kinau (top) and Keoneoio (bottom) are today frequented only by hikers and fishermen.

Aerial photography is my favorite. I like the perspectives of color and design that become apparent from the air.

I also like the feeling of flying, especially in a helicopter. You spot things you never noticed before, although you may have driven past them a hundred times. This is particularly true of Maui where the roads tend to hug the coast. From the air, you see how big and varied the island really is.

All of the photos in this book with the exception of a few ground shots were taken from helicopters. The most important part of aerial photography is finding good pilots. I had the help of several in this project—Chuck Whiteman of AG Helicopters, Don Ballard of Hawaii Helicopters, Zac Baricuarto of Kenai Air, Inc., and H. D. "Woody" Wood and Bob Stanga of Makani Kai Helicopters. I am in their debt for their ability, patience and knowledge of the island.

Of secondary importance is equipment. Most of the photography was done with a Pentax 67 medium-format camera. Some smaller photos and ground shots were made with 35 mm Nikons.

Of course, good weather is important, too. But that's really not hard to find on Maui where almost every day presents opportunities for the camera. In fact, Maui is one of the best places I know to tour by air. In an hour you see incredible beaches, tropical rain forests, more waterfalls than you can count, and even the lunarlike landscape of Haleakala.

Douglas Peebles

Produced by Bennett Hymer
Photography by Douglas Peebles
Text by Tom Stevens
Editorial Assistance by
  Stuart Lillico
Corporate Liaison:
  Gaylen Wong

Art Direction and Design by
  Fred Bechlen and
  Leo Gonzalez
Design Assistants:
  Gail Campbell and
  Lilia Chua
Maps: Christine Wilhite/
  Time2Design

Typeset by Typehouse Hawaii
Headlines: Futura Black
Text: Baskerville Roman
Captions: Baskerville Italic

Printed and Bound in Taiwan